SPORTS ZONE

GYMNASTICS
A Guide for Athletes and Fans

BY MATT CHANDLER

raintree
a Capstone company — publishers for children

Raintree is an imprint of Capstone Global Library Limited, a company incorporated in England and Wales having its registered office at 264 Banbury Road, Oxford, OX2 7DY – Registered company number: 6695582

www.raintree.co.uk
myorders@raintree.co.uk

Edited by Lauren Dupuis-Perez
Designed by Sara Radka
Original illustrations © Capstone Global Library Limited 2020
Picture research by Eric Gohl
Production by Laura Manthe
Originated by Capstone Global Library Ltd
Printed and bound in India

978 1 4747 8877 9 (hardback)
978 1 4747 8879 3 (paperback)

British Library Cataloguing in Publication Data
A full catalogue record for this book is available from the British Library.

Acknowledgements
We would like to thank the following for permission to reproduce photographs: Getty Images: Allsport/Doug Pensinger, 22, Dan Mullan, 11 (#5), Ezra Shaw, cover (foreground), Francois Nel, 4, 11 (#3, 4, 6, 7), Image Source, 29, (top), Jed Jacobsohn, 25, Lars Baron, 20, M_a_y_a, cover (background), Mike Powell, 23, Phil Walter, 19, Quinn Rooney, 12, Ronald Martinez, 24, Steve Powell, 7, Tim Bradbury, 10, (bottom), Tom Pennington, 14; Pixabay: intographics, background; Newscom: Mitchell Reibel, 9; Shutterstock: Abdo Allam, 17, Jan von Uxkull-Gyllenband, 10, (top), Leonard Zhukovsky, 29, (bottom), muratart, 11 (#8), Nataliya Turpitko, 28, Polhansen, 8–9, roibu, 10-11 (background), UfaBizPhoto, 27; Wikimedia: Daniel Chodowiecki, 6, Unknown, 13

CONTENTS

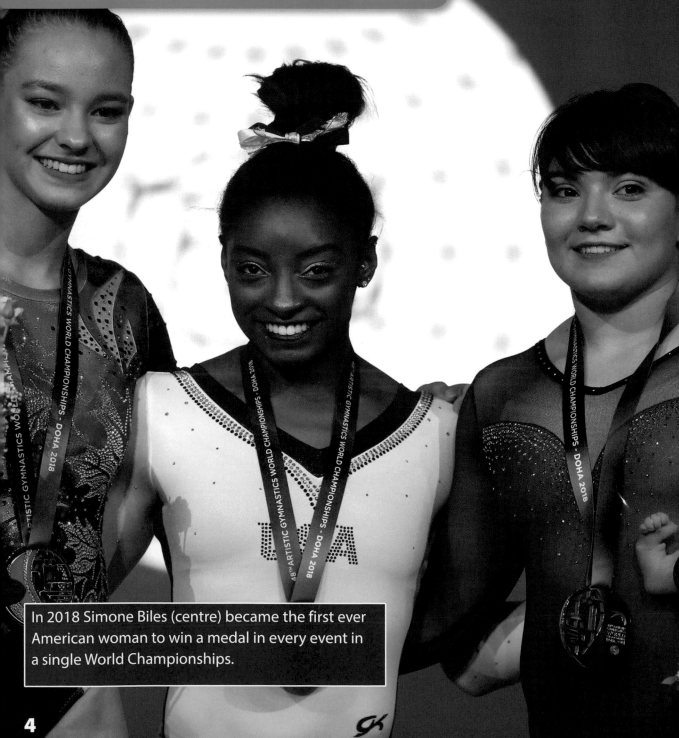

In 2018 Simone Biles (centre) became the first ever American woman to win a medal in every event in a single World Championships.

The crowd in the Olympic arena in Rio de Janeiro erupted as US gymnast Simone Biles stuck her final landing. Even before her scores were in, the smile on Biles' face told the story. The 19-year-old had just won Olympic gold in the floor exercise at the 2016 Summer Olympics! Biles left Brazil with five Olympic medals. She earned a place in history as one of the best gymnasts ever.

Gymnastics is an exciting sport. It combines strength, grace and **acrobatics**. Beginners in tumbling classes learn the basics. Junior competitors improve their skills by competing against other gymnasts. The very best athletes earn a chance to compete in international events such as the Olympics. No matter what level they compete at, all gymnasts share a love of performing and training to be the very best they can be.

acrobatics movements that require good balance, agility and coordination

GYMNASTICS HISTORY

Johann
Bernhard Basedow

Have you ever noticed how muscular people are in ancient Greek sculptures? The Greeks owe some of that to their dedication to early gymnastics. Gymnastics was part of the exercise routine of Greek men as early as the 8th century BC. Tumbling and vaulting are two examples of gymnastic events that began in ancient times.

In 1774, a German teacher called Johann Bernhard Basedow reintroduced gymnastics to the modern sports world. He took many of the Greek exercises and expanded on them. With the sport's rise in popularity came the invention of the parallel bars, the balance beam and tumbling.

Gymnastics was part of the first modern Olympics. The games were held in Greece in 1896. Men competed in events including rings, vault and the pommel horse. They could also medal in rope climbing! Greek gymnast Nikolaos Andriakopoulos won the gold in this unusual event. It was dropped as an Olympic event after the 1932 games.

At the 1984 Summer Olympics, Mary Lou Retton (third from right) scored a perfect 10.0 in two events: the vault and the floor exercise.

Athletes from Europe and the Soviet Union **dominated** the sport for decades. It wasn't until the 1984 Summer Olympics in Los Angeles, California, that athletes from North America began to emerge as superstars on the world stage. Led by Mary Lou Retton and Julianne McNamara, the United States earned its first-ever Olympic gold medals in gymnastics.

dominate rule; in sport, a team or person dominates if they win much more than anyone else

Not every gymnast aims to compete in the Olympics. Many enjoy gymnastics for the teamwork and friendship. Others compete on school teams. Some gymnasts join local clubs and compete against other clubs in regional competitions. The best gymnasts train year-round and travel the world, competing against top-level competitors. They are the athletes with the goal to represent their nation in the Olympics and world **championships**.

NO UNIFORM NEEDED!

In ancient Greece, gymnastics was called *gymnazein*, which means "train naked". Exercise was important to the Greeks. They believed in showing off the results of their hard work!

championship contest or tournament that decides which team is the best

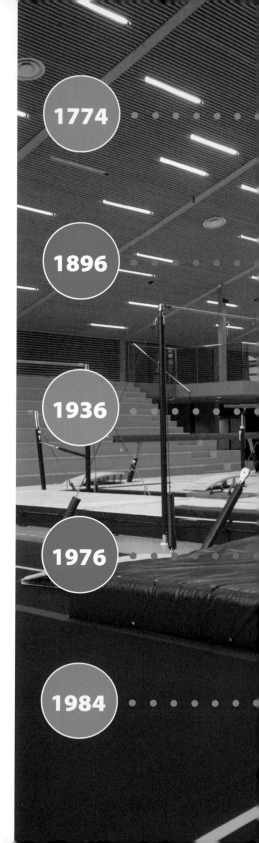

1774

1896

1936

1976

1984

Johann Bernhard Basedow introduces exercise in his school in Germany. This is considered to be the birth of modern gymnastics.

Men's gymnastics is officially included in the first Olympic Games in Athens, Greece.

Women's gymnastics is added to the Olympics but is limited to the all-around competition.

At the Summer Games in Montreal, Canada, Romanian gymnast Nadia Comăneci earns the first perfect score in Olympic gymnastics history.

Mary Lou Retton becomes the first American woman to win all-around gold in the history of the Olympics.

Golden girl

In the summer of 1984, Mary Lou Retton became a role model for young gymnasts around the world. Retton earned five medals at the 1984 Olympics. That was more than any athlete that year.

Retton retired from competitive gymnastics in 1986. She went on to appear in films and TV series. She worked as a television commentator for gymnastics. She even competed on the US version of *Strictly Come Dancing: Dancing with the Stars*.

ESSENTIAL EQUIPMENT

Geared for gold

Brazilian gymnast Arthur Zanetti looked up at the two rings hanging more than 2.4 metres (8 feet) above his head. With a boost, he grabbed the wooden rings and began his routine.

The two rings hung from cables approximately 3 metres (10 feet) long. Flipping between the straps took precision, timing and concentration. One wrong move and he could lose his grip and fall. Instead, Zanetti executed a near-perfect routine and won the men's gold at the 2016 Summer Olympics.

SHARED EVENTS

1. Vault
Gymnasts sprint down a runway roughly 25 metres (82 feet) long and hurdle onto a springboard that launches them in the air. They spring off a vaulting table that is set 135 cm (4 feet 5 inches) off the floor for men and 125 cm (4 feet 3 inches) off the floor for women. They perform a complicated flip and stick a landing.

2. Floor exercise mat
Gymnasts show off their best flips, leaps and twists on a mat that is 12 m (40 feet) by 12 m.

MEN'S EVENTS

3. Pommel horse

Male gymnasts hold onto two handles, called pommels, and perform routines by swinging their bodies around the horse.

4. Rings

Regulation rings are 18 cm (7 inches) in diameter and hang from nylon straps 2.8 m (9.2 feet) above the floor.

5. Parallel bars

Two bars are set 2 metres (6 feet 4 inches) high and 42 cm (16.5 inches) apart. Athletes perform a wide range of swinging acrobatic moves on the bars.

6. Horizontal bar

Athletes swing and flip from this single steel bar set roughly 2.7 metres (9 feet) off the floor. Routines end with a dismount onto a mat.

WOMEN'S EVENTS

7. Balance beam

Gymnasts perform complex routines on the 4.9-metre (16-foot) balance beam. They dance, leap and flip on a beam only 10 centimetres (4 inches) wide and 1.2 m (4 feet) above the floor!

8. Uneven parallel bars

Gymnasts perform dazzling flips on bars set at different heights and distances from each other. The height varies at different levels of competition.

regulation follows an official rule

Clothing

Today, uniforms worn by gymnasts combine fashion with performance. Gymnasts perform incredible routines. They want to look good doing it. The 2016 American women's team in Rio de Janeiro, Brazil, wore **leotards** designed with nearly 5,000 crystals! Gymnasts' uniforms must also be designed to move with their bodies. That means tight suits that cut down on wind resistance as gymnasts leap, spin and jump. Women gymnasts wear leotards that are high-cut in order to free their legs.

On the men's side, the uniform depends on the event. Many competitors wear special trousers and vests. The trousers are specially designed to come down over their feet. This protects the gymnast from catching his trouser leg on a piece of equipment such as a pommel horse. Others wear more typical shorts and tops.

Lauren Hernandez and her US teammates at the 2016 Olympics were as much in the news for their sparkly leotards as their gymnastics. Each leotard had about 5,000 Swarovski crystals on them!

Leaping, flipping and swinging from all of this equipment can be dangerous. Sweaty hands or feet can cause a gymnast to slip or lose their grip. The tiniest slip can cause the judges to take away points from an athlete's score. A fall can ruin an event or lead to a potential injury.

Before gymnasts begin routines on the vault, for example, they dig their hands into a bowl next to the mat. It is filled with chalk. To be safe, athletes use plenty of chalk to dry up moisture from sweat.

GIDDY UP

The "horse" used in pommel horse events can be traced back more than 2,000 years. Alexander the Great used pommel horses to train his soldiers to mount real horses.

leotard tight-fitting, one-piece garment worn by dancers and gymnasts

Aly Raisman's favourite gymnastics event is the floor exercise. She won gold in the event at the 2012 Olympics and silver at the 2016 games.

In a sport where athletes are often separated by a fraction of a point, following the rules is important. Just ask the 1988 US and German Women's Olympic teams. The US squad lost the bronze medal by 0.3 of a point to Germany. During the competition, the Americans were penalized for a rules violation and half a point was deducted. Olympic alternate Rhonda Faehn remained on the platform while her US teammate, Kelly Garrison-Steves, performed her routine. That may not seem important, but it was against the rules. It cost the Americans a medal.

With so many different events in gymnastics, each **apparatus** has a unique set of rules. The rules of the pommel horse are different from the uneven parallel bars. An athlete competing on the floor exercise has different rules from on the balance beam. With most gymnasts competing in multiple events, understanding the rules for each is important.

apparatus equipment used by gymnasts when they perform

Rules for men's competition

Men and women compete in several different gymnastic events at the competitive level. The only shared events are vault and floor. Men's gymnastics offers six events. They are floor exercise, pommel horse, rings, vault, parallel bars and the high bar.

The **compulsory** rules across the shared events differ per group. Men's floor routines typically focus on tumbling, to display strength. The vault table is the same for both groups. However, it is set higher for men's competitions. The exact height depends on the level of competition. The men's parallel bars event is unique because of the apparatus used. Men compete on parallel bars that are about 46 cm (18 inches) apart. Judges focus on the athlete's strength and agility on the bars as they perform their routine.

compulsory something that is required

Japanese gymnast Kohei Uchimura won the men's all-round competition at the 2016 Olympic Games.

Rules for women's competition

Women's gymnastics includes four competitive events. They are vault, uneven bars, balance beam and the floor exercise.

One unique element sets apart the floor exercise for women. In addition to powerful tumbling, women's floor routines are also judged on elements of dance and grace. To demonstrate rhythm, they perform to music. Men do not.

For the uneven bars, women perform a more acrobatic routine to fly between two uneven bars. In both events, as with all gymnastics events, emphasis is placed on executing a perfect landing or dismount.

Restrictive rules

Gabby Douglas has three Olympic gold medals. In the 2016 Summer Games, Douglas lost a chance for a fourth thanks to a restrictive rule. To make sure one country doesn't dominate an event, the Olympics enforce a "two per country" rule. No country can have more than two athletes advance in an event. Americans Simone Biles, Aly Raisman and Douglas finished at the top in the all-around competition. But because of the rule, Douglas was eliminated.

Beth Tweddle is Britain's most successful ever female gymnast. She won a bronze in the uneven bars at the 2012 London Olympics.

Beyond those few differences, the rules for both competitions are the same. The size of the team and the rules to qualify at events are the same for men and women. All teams have four members. In both groups, judges score using the same point system, with 10.0 being a perfect score.

RULES VIOLATION

In the 2000 Olympics in Australia, several athletes struggled on the vault. Officials measured the height. They found it was 5 centimetres (2 inches) shorter than regulation.

STRATEGIES TO SUCCEED

Flávia Saraiva of Brazil took fifth place in the balance beam at the 2016 Olympics. She is 133 cm (4 feet) tall and weighs less than 32 kilograms (70 pounds).

Flávia Saraiva is in the Olympic record books even though she didn't win a medal in 2016. When she stepped to the mat in her native Brazil for the Summer Olympics, Saraiva became one of the shortest Olympic gymnasts in history at only 133 cm (4 feet) tall. Many of the women who compete are under 152 cm (5 feet). Gold medallist US gymnast Simone Biles is 142 cm (4 feet, 8 inches). Some **experts** believe there is science behind the success of short gymnasts.

A small object takes less energy to move. Some people believe that the smaller you are, the less muscle you require to perform. Muscle is heavy. Less muscle means less weight. That makes it easier to fly gracefully through the air and land a perfect dismount. There are plenty of tall gymnasts. But science suggests there is an advantage to being small.

expert person with great skill or a lot of knowledge of a subject

Brain boost

It takes dedication, hard work, and talent to become a top gymnast. It also takes mental toughness. Kerri Strug demonstrated her toughness in front of the world. In the 1996 Summer Games, Strug badly injured her ankle on the landing of her first vault attempt. She could barely walk, but her team needed her to perform one more routine. Though only a teenager, Strug blocked out the pain and returned to the runway. She delivered a heroic performance and led her team to the gold medal. Strug had to be carried from the arena, unable to walk on her ankle. Her mental toughness allowed her to fight against the odds and earn the gold.

Kerri Strug was 18 years old at the time of the 1996 Olympic Games. She attended her first Olympics in 1992 at the age of 14.

Coach Béla Károlyi carried Kerri Strug onto the podium for the medal ceremony of the 1996 Olympics gymnastics competition.

Olympic gymnasts must overcome poor performances. They must recover from injuries and face their fears. Being mentally strong is as important as having natural talent.

Dong Dong earned China a medal in trampoline at each of the 2008, 2012 and 2016 Olympic Games.

Practice for perfection

Chinese gymnast Dong Dong executed a flawless triple somersault on the trampoline at the 2012 Olympics on his way to winning the gold medal. It is the type of move that takes hours of practice to perfect. Fans only see athletes perform. They don't see the years spent in gyms perfecting their routines.

A panel of judges watches every move a gymnast makes. The slightest error can be the difference between victory or defeat. That's why gymnasts dedicate so many hours to practice.

Mary Lou Retton practised up to 70 vaults every day in preparation for the 1984 Olympics. Aly Raisman (see page 29) once said, "You kind of have to push yourself to the point where you feel you can do your routine in your sleep." A gymnastics routine involves several moves that must be perfectly timed. As all top gymnasts know, practice really does make perfect.

(see page 29)

AGELESS WONDER

Incredible training and thousands of hours of practice paid off for Oksana Chusovitina. The Russian gymnast set a record competing in seven consecutive Olympics, including in 2016 at the age of 41.

Oksana Chusovitina has earned one gold and one silver medal in Olympic competition.

Does gymnastics sound like fun? The good news is, getting started can be easy. Your school or local leisure centre probably offers classes in gymnastics that are great for beginners. Children can also sign up for classes at private gyms that specialize in gymnastics. There you will train with coaches who are usually former gymnasts.

This is a great way to learn the basics of the sport. You will begin by exploring the different types of gymnastics and the importance of safety. This can be a great chance to decide what type of gymnastics you like. Some beginners enjoy the graceful techniques of a floor routine. Others want to experience the heart-pounding thrill of the balance beam or the parallel bars. Taking lessons can help you decide which events are right for you.

You can try the different types of gymnastics available at a club, local leisure centre or at school.

Take it to the next level

For young gymnasts who want to perform competitively, be prepared to practise – a lot. Gold medallist Simone Biles says she practised 32 hours a week to prepare for the Olympics. Imagine how sore your muscles will be after running, tumbling and flipping for 32 hours!

The Olympics are held every four years. A typical gymnast trains between five and eight years to make it to the world's biggest stage. Competitive gymnastics can also be expensive. The cost goes up as athletes rise in the ranks of competitive gymnastics.

Gymnastics is a great way to stay fit and flexible!

FUN FOR ALL AGES

Johanna Quaas took her first gymnastics class in her 50s. At the age of 86, she was recognized by Guinness World Records as the oldest gymnast in the world.

If long hours in the gym and sore muscles don't scare you away, competitive gymnastics can be an amazing experience. You'll make friends, be part of a team and have a chance to travel. And maybe, just maybe, you'll find yourself on the podium one day receiving your own medal!

Gymnasts often train 20 to 30 hours a week, but even a few hours a week can improve your strength, flexibility and overall health.

Starting young

Three-time Olympic gold medallist Aly Raisman began her gymnastics career when she was just 2 years old! By the time she turned 10, Raisman was a veteran gymnast with plans for the future. She began training harder than ever before. Her hard work paid off. In 2012, Raisman qualified for the Summer Olympics in London, where she won three medals! Raisman added three more medals at the 2016 games in Brazil.

Glossary

acrobatics movements that require good balance, agility and coordination

apparatus equipment used by gymnasts when they perform

championship contest or tournament that decides which team is the best

compulsory something that is required

dominate to rule; in sport, a team or person dominates if they win much more than anyone else

expert person with great skill or a lot of knowledge of a subject

leotard tight-fitting, one-piece garment worn by dancers and gymnasts

regulation follows an official rule

Find out more

Books

Floor Exercise: Tips, Rules and Legendary Stars, Heather E. Schwartz (Raintree, 2017)

Gymnastics (Usborne Spectator Guides), Sam Lake and Emily Bone (Usborne, 2016)

The Science Behind Gymnastics (Science of the Summer Olympics), L.E. Carmichael (Raintree, 2016)

Websites

www.bbc.com/bitesize/articles/z36j7ty

www.british-gymnastics.org

www.dkfindout.com/uk/sports/gymnastics

Index